kids

PRAYING FOR KIDS

Volume IV

This prayer journal belongs to:

Published by Tommy Nelson®, a Division of Thomas Nelson, Inc.,
P.O. Box 141000, Nashville, Tennessee 37214.

Unless otherwise noted, scriptures quoted from the International Children's Bible®, New Century Version®,
copyright © 1986, 1988, 1999 by Tommy Nelson®, a Division of Thomas Nelson, Inc.,
Nashville, Tennessee 37214. Used by permission.
Scriptures noted (NKJV) are taken from the New King James Version.
Copyright © 1979, 1980, 1982 by Thomas Nelson, Inc. Used by permission. All rights reserved.
Scriptures noted (NIV) are taken from the HOLY BIBLE, NEW INTERNATIONAL VERSION.
Copyright © 1973, 1978, 1984 International Bible Society.
Used by permission of Zondervan Bible Publishers.

ISBN 1-4003-0197-1

Printed in Peru
03 04 05 06 QWQ 5 4 3 2 1

Samaritan's Purse™
INTERNATIONAL RELIEF

INTERNATIONAL HEADQUARTERS
P.O. Box 3000
Boone, NC 28607-3000
(828) 262-1980

AUSTRALIA
Samaritan's Purse – Australia, Ltd.
Box 6544
Blacktown Business Centre
NSW 2148
(02) 9676 4055

CANADA
Samaritan's Purse – Canada
Box 20100, Calgary Place
Calgary, AB T2P 4J2
(800) 663-6500

GERMANY
Geschenke der Hoffnung e.V.
Haynauer Strasse 72a
D-12249 Berlin
0180 577 577-1

IRELAND
Samaritan's Purse – Ireland
Gledswood Lodge
Bird Avenue
Clonskeagh
Dublin 14
(01) 269 5055

NETHERLANDS
De Barmhartige Samaritaan
Schoolpad 1B
3851 JE Ermelo
(31) 341-418061

UNITED KINGDOM
Samaritan's Purse International, Ltd.
Victoria House, Victoria Road
Buckhurst Hill, Essex 1G9 5EX
(020) 8559 2044

www.samaritanspurse.org

kids

PRAYING FOR KIDS

A 12-MONTH PRAYER JOURNEY AROUND THE WORLD

NELSON

www.tommynelson.com

A Division of Thomas Nelson, Inc.
www.ThomasNelson.com

This Prayer Journal Is Dedicated To Ruth Bell Graham

Growing up as the daughter of missionaries to China, Ruth Bell Graham learned how to pray at an early age. As a mother, she taught her own children to pray always—not just when they were in trouble!

Since her own children have grown up, she has continued to help other children around the world understand that Jesus loves them and that they can talk to Him about everything. Her love and kindness are a great example to everyone she meets.

Prayer: A Great Adventure

Ever since I was a small boy, I have always loved a good adventure. I would spend hours with my dogs exploring the hills and woods around my family's mountain log cabin, sometimes even camping out underneath the stars. Those days were fun, but I am so thankful that my parents introduced me to an even more exciting and rewarding adventure—prayer.

Can you imagine the great ways God can use us if we just ask Him? My mother taught me that prayer was simply talking and listening to God. I am sure that you know God created the universe, our world, and each one of us. But did you know that God loves for us to talk to Him, and He loves to answer us? And no matter where you are, your prayers can reach around the world. Now that's an adventure!

I work for Samaritan's Purse, and we travel the world looking for people who need help, much like the Good Samaritan in the Bible (read Luke 10:25-37). You'll learn about some of the children we've met as you read this book. If you want, you can help them too! All you have to do is pray. It may sound simple, but it's an important and powerful thing you can do.

Prayer doesn't just change the world. It can change you, too. I hope this book will help you begin a long and exciting journey as you learn to talk and listen to God, and I pray that He will begin to work in you and show you how much He loves you. May God bless you on this great adventure!

Your friend,
Franklin Graham

kids

PRAYING FOR KIDS

A 12-MONTH PRAYER JOURNEY AROUND THE WORLD

As you pray for the children mentioned each month, find where they live on this map of the world. An easy way to do this is to match the flags of the countries shown on this page with the flag of the country featured each month. Use the list of countries below to write the name of the country in the blank beside the flag.

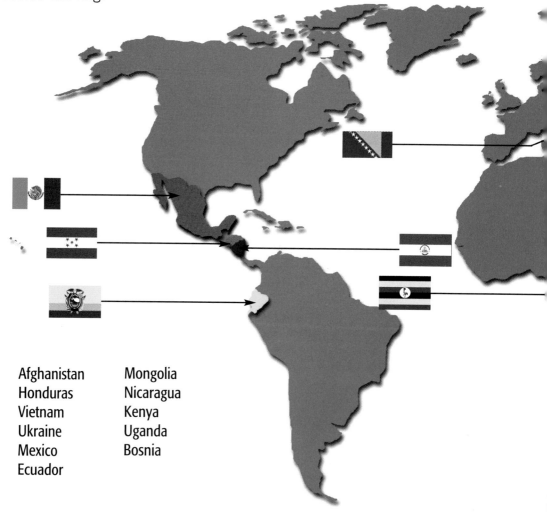

Afghanistan
Honduras
Vietnam
Ukraine
Mexico
Ecuador

Mongolia
Nicaragua
Kenya
Uganda
Bosnia

How to use this journal:

1. Plan to spend time each day talking to God and writing in your prayer journal. You might want to do this first thing in the morning or just before you go to bed at night.

2. Pay special attention to the Bible verse for each month. Read it each day and think about what it means. Set a goal of memorizing the verse (and maybe even some others) every month.

3. Pray each day for that month's prayer requests, along with your own list of concerns. Write them in your prayer journal, and note God's answers to earlier prayers. Be sure to write down things that you're thankful for, too.

4. As the year goes along, read back through your prayer journal. It will remind you of God's goodness and of things you may want to keep praying about.

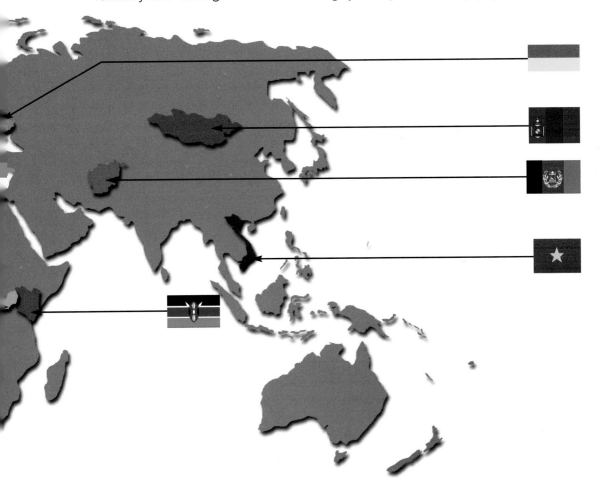

Pray for the Kids in
Afghanistan

Discover Afghanistan

Size: 249,700 square miles
(slightly smaller than Texas)
Population: 27,755,775
Capital City: Kabul (KA-bool)

Ten-year-old Bibi lost her mother, her father, and her little brother when their home was destroyed in the recent fighting in Afghanistan. Bibi was away from home when her family was killed, but she was rescued by strangers who helped her find a place to live in a tent city.

When the Samaritan's Purse team brought blankets, shoes, stoves, and food to the people living in tents, Bibi asked for a pen and paper. The next time the team came, Bibi showed them a picture of a child flying a kite with tanks and missiles all around. Flying kites had been against the law, but now she can fly her kite in her new home.

Thousands of other boys and girls in Afghanistan are finally going back to class after Samaritan's Purse helped rebuild their schools. They have seen that God cares for them. They can now hope for many more days to fly their kites.

- Pray for Afghan children who live in tents through cold winters.

- Pray that people in Afghanistan will hear the Good News of Jesus Christ.

How to Make a Square Kite (Afghanistan Style)

You will need:
- 1 sheet of construction paper
- Ball of string
- Strips of paper

Step 1: Fold an 8 1/2" x 11" sheet of paper in half. Draw a line across the paper 1 inch from the fold. Fold back and forth on the line.

Step 2: With the folded side closest to you, draw a dot 3 inches from the left side and 3/4" from the bottom. Make a hole through the dot by putting tape on top of it, then poking a hole through both layers. Run a piece of string through the hole and tie.

Step 3: Holding the bottom fold closed, open the paper and tape the bottom fold closed.

Step 4: Mark 1 inch from the top on the left side, and draw a line across. Tape a soda straw on the line.

Step 5: Make a tail out of paper, cutting the ends into thin strips. Tape each strip together to make one long piece, and attach it on the end opposite of the straw.

Now go fly your kite!

My Prayer List

_____
_____
_____
_____
_____
_____
_____
_____

God, Thank You For . . .

_____
_____
_____
_____
_____
_____
_____

Answers To My Prayers

_____
_____
_____

FEBRUARY

Pray for the Kids in
Honduras

Discover Honduras

Size: 43,100 square miles
(about the size of Virginia)

Population: 6,560,608

Capital City: Tegucigalpa
(te-goo-see-GAL-pah)

Do you like to drink milk with cookies? Can you imagine having no milk to drink at all? Eight-year-old Marilyn had not tasted milk since she was a baby. Then one day, Samaritan's Purse brought goats to her village in Honduras. When she saw the goats, Marilyn called out, "Oh, Mommy, now we can drink milk!"

Each family in the village received a female goat. That meant they could have a gallon of milk every day—plenty for the children to drink and to make butter and cheese. Most of these goats produce two baby goats a year, and families can sell them for money to live on.

Now Marilyn has a goat to play with and milk to drink every day—thanks to Samaritan's Purse.

- Pray that more children in Honduras will receive the food they need to grow healthy.

- Pray that people in Honduras will turn to their heavenly Father to meet their needs.

Bible Verse for February

If one of you says to him, "Go, I wish you well; keep warm and well fed," but does nothing about his physical needs, what good is it? James 2:16 (NIV)

How to Make Honduran Clay Marbles

You will need:

- Modeling clay
- Tempura or acrylic paints and a brush
- Tapered-end toothpicks
- A wooden surface or plastic cloth to work on

Step 1: Knead the clay on a wooden surface or plastic cloth.

Step 2: Break off about a teaspoonful and roll into a round ball.

Step 3: Repeat to make as many marbles as you want.

Step 4: Insert a toothpick into each and let dry thoroughly.

Step 5: Holding a marble by the toothpick, paint each with your own design. Be creative!

Step 6: Let dry and gently remove toothpick.

My Prayer List

_____
_____
_____
_____
_____
_____
_____
_____

God, Thank You For . . .

_____
_____
_____
_____
_____
_____
_____
_____

Answers To My Prayers

_____
_____
_____

MARCH

Pray for the Kids in
Vietnam

Discover Vietnam

Size: 125,500 square miles
(slightly larger than New Mexico)
Population: 81,098,415
Capital City: Hanoi (HA-noy)

Since he was born, Dat has not been able to hear or talk. He lived with his grandmother who sold tea beside the road to make money so they both could eat. Some nights tea was all they had for a meal.

But good things started to happen when Dat went to a school for street children, which Samaritan's Purse helps operate. Dat learned to make carvings out of soapstone. Now, after only one year, he carves beautiful designs and animals using only his senses of touch and sight.

Many people want to buy a soapstone carving by Dat. They often place special orders for what they want. Best of all, Dat earns enough from selling his carvings to support his grandmother and himself.

- Pray for children in Vietnam who do not have a home of any kind and must live on the streets.

- Pray that children will feel the love of Jesus Christ even when they do not have others to love them.

Bible Verse for March

But Lord, you are our father. We are like clay, and you are the potter.
Your hands made us all. Isaiah 64:8

How to Make a "Soapstone" Carving

You will need:

- Modeling clay
- Large paper clip
- Cup of water

Step 1: Take a ball of clay, about 3 to 5 inches in diameter, and work it until soft.

Step 2: Roll it into a rock-like shape.

Step 3: Using your fingers, form an animal from the clay.

Step 4: Smooth your carving, using your finger dipped in water.

Step 5: Use the big paper clip to make facial features and add other details (stripes or spots, for example).

Step 6: Let the animal dry completely.

You might want to make a whole zoo!

My Prayer List

_____
_____
_____
_____
_____
_____
_____
_____

God, Thank You For . . .

_____
_____
_____
_____
_____
_____
_____

Answers To My Prayers

_____
_____
_____
_____

APRIL

Pray for the Kids in
Ukraine

Discover Ukraine

Size: 233,089 square miles
(slightly smaller than Texas)
Population: 48,396,470
Capital City: Kiev (KEY-yev)

Anton didn't have a lot to smile about. His family was very poor, and he was born with a condition called cerebral palsy. He could not control his muscles or walk. Anton had to use a wheelchair and stayed at home most of the time.

Anton was ten when his mother brought him to a church in Kiev, the city where they lived. It was December and already very cold. They had heard that Christmas gifts from Samaritan's Purse would be given out to children. When the pastor handed a bright red-and-green box to Anton, a huge smile spread across his face. His mother said it was the happiest she had ever seen Anton.

Three years later, Anton leads a small Bible study group and wants to be a pastor when he grows up. Now many people see Anton smile as he talks about the love of Jesus.

- Pray for children who cannot walk where they want to go.

- Pray that many more children in Ukraine will learn the joy of God's love.

Bible Verse for April

This is the day that the Lord has made. Let us rejoice and be glad today!
Psalm 118:24

How to Make Pysanky (PIE-san-key) (Ukrainian Easter Eggs)

You will need:

- Boiled white eggs that have been cooled
- Brightly colored dyes
- Small bowls or cups to hold the dyes
- Brushes for applying egg dye
- Melted beeswax or a white crayon
- A candle

Step 1: Use a lead pencil to draw a design or simple picture such as a cross on the egg.

Step 2: Cover all the areas you want to remain white with wax.

Step 3: Dip your egg into a colored dye, such as yellow.

Step 4: Cover all of the parts of the egg you wish to remain yellow with wax, and dip the egg into another color, such as red. Continue to do this with as many designs and colors as you want. Make designs to stay a certain color by covering with the wax before dipping into a new color.

Step 5: When you are finished dyeing the egg, have an adult hold the egg over a lighted candle, rotate the egg, and wipe the wax off the egg with a soft cloth as it melts.

My Prayer List

_____
_____
_____
_____
_____
_____
_____
_____

God, Thank You For . . .

_____
_____
_____
_____
_____
_____
_____

Answers To My Prayers

_____
_____
_____
_____

Pray for the Kids in
Mexico

Discover Mexico

Size: 741,600 square miles
(as big as Alaska plus Nebraska)
Population: 103,400,165
Capital City: Mexico City

Do you ever thank God for the roof over your head? Many children and their families near Merida, Mexico, do it very often now. Last September a strong hurricane hit their country and, literally, took the roofs off their homes. Because of the storm's heavy rains, the farmers in the region lost much of the food they planted and the animals they were raising.

The churches around Merida decided to help their needy neighbors. Samaritan's Purse joined them, and together they provided food for these hungry families. They also got to work fixing their roofs, so the boys and girls and their parents could have a warm, dry place to live again.

Samaritan's Purse and the local Christians showed Jesus' love to these families through good deeds. Now many people in Merida know that if they build their lives on the Lord Jesus Christ, no storm can wash away their hope.

- Pray that more families in Mexico would build their lives on the solid rock of Jesus Christ.

- Pray that God would use your good deeds to show others how much He loves them.

Bible Verse for May

In the same way, you should be a light for other people. Live so that they will see the good things you do and will praise your Father in heaven. Matthew 5:16

How to Make a Mexican Piñata

You will need:

- A large paper grocery bag
- Several bags of individually wrapped candies
- Hole puncher
- Tissue paper
- Stapler, glue, and scissors

Step 1: Fill the grocery bag about halfway full of candies. Fold the top down tightly and staple the fold. Punch two holes in the top just under the fold.

Step 2: Decorate the bag with an animal face, feathers, or buttons.

Step 3: Cut narrow strips of brightly colored tissue paper and glue all around the bag. Glue long strips to the bottom of the bag so they will hang down.

Step 4: Lace a long string through the holes in the top of the bag, and get an adult to help tie your piñata about 4 feet from the floor.

Step 5: Blindfold one of the players, give him or her a stick, turn the player around and around, and let him try to break the piñata!

Enjoy the candies!

My Prayer List

_____

_____

_____

_____

_____

_____

_____

_____

God, Thank You For . . .

_____

_____

_____

_____

_____

_____

_____

Answers To My Prayers

_____

_____

_____

_____

JUNE

Pray for the Kids in
Ecuador

Discover Ecuador

Size: 104,550 square miles
(about the size of Nevada)
Population: 13,447,498
Capital City: Quito (key-TOE)

Many children who need to hear about Jesus live in places where airplanes cannot land. One such place is the Amazon rainforest in Ecuador. Last year, Samaritan's Purse workers traveled four hours up the Rio Napo River with a motor canoe loaded with gift-filled shoe boxes for children in a primitive tribe in the rainforest. This tribe had once been savage warriors.

The river was flooded and swift, but the Samaritan's Purse workers docked the canoe and began their work. While the workers were delivering the shoe boxes, the fierce current slammed a big floating log into their canoe and sank it—right after they had unloaded all the shoe boxes!

- Pray for the children of Ecuador who received shoe box gifts, that they would know God's greatest gift, His Son, Jesus Christ.

- Pray that Samaritan's Purse would be able to show God's love to people all across South America.

How to Make an Ecuadorian Fiesta Headdress

You will need:

- Two large sheets of construction paper
- Crayons and markers
- Glue
- Glitter, feathers, ribbons, and buttons
- Stapler

Step 1: Using the sheets of paper, cut out two U shapes. Make sure they are wide enough to fit around your head.

Step 2: Draw designs or pictures on the paper shapes with crayons or markers.

Step 3: Glue on glitter, bright buttons, feathers, or fabric scraps. Let dry.

Step 4: After the glue has dried, staple the two shapes together at the bottom corners and a few inches up the sides.

Step 5: Staple on ribbons or more dangling feathers and wear.

Now have a fiesta!

My Prayer List

_____
_____
_____
_____
_____
_____
_____
_____

God, Thank You For . . .

_____
_____
_____
_____
_____
_____
_____
_____

Answers To My Prayers

_____
_____
_____
_____

Pray for the Kids in
Mongolia

Discover Mongolia
Size: 603,500 square miles
(larger than Alaska)
Population: 2,694,432
Capital City: Ulaanbaatar
(oo-lon-bah-TAR)

Munkhuu lives in a felt tent with her parents and two sisters. She was only a toddler when her family discovered she had a heart problem. They were worried because her older brother had died with a similar heart defect. Doctors knew Munkhuu needed an operation as soon as possible, but there were no heart surgeons in Mongolia to help her.

The Samaritan's Purse Children's Heart Project flew both Munkhuu and her mother to Canada. There, a team of doctors was waiting to operate on Munkhuu, free of charge. They were able to fix her heart, and now Munkhuu is a changed girl.

Munkhuu's mother is also a changed person. Through the love of the Christian family they stayed with in Canada, she came to believe in Jesus and was baptized before she and Munkhuu returned home to Mongolia.

• Pray for the children in Mongolia who need special help from doctors because of serious health problems.

• Pray that more children and their families will know Jesus Christ as the "Great Physician" who heals their hearts with love.

Bible Verse for July

Therefore confess your sins to each other and pray for each other so that you may be healed. The prayer of a righteous man is powerful and effective. James 5:16 (NIV)

How to Make a Felt Pincushion

You will need:

- A piece of felt about 8 by 10 inches
- A roll of steel wool
- Glue
- Scissors
- Magic markers

Step 1: Fold the felt in half and cut along the fold.

Step 2: Using a round object such as a saucer, mark a circle on each piece of felt.

Step 3: Cut out the circles.

Step 4: Flatten and stretch the steel wool to fit between the circles.

Step 5: Glue around the edge of the bottom circle and press the edge of the top circle down into the glue until the two hold together.

Step 6: When dry, decorate the pincushion with magic markers.

My Prayer List

_____
_____
_____
_____
_____
_____
_____

God, Thank You For . . .

_____
_____
_____
_____
_____
_____

Answers To My Prayers

_____
_____
_____

AUGUST

Pray for the Kids in
Nicaragua

Discover Nicaragua

Size: 46,400 square miles
(the size of Pennsylvania)

Population: 5,023,818

Capital City: Managua
(muh-NAH-gwuh)

C ould you lead worship in your church? That's what a ten-year-old boy named Israel Eliut Hernandez does in his hometown in Nicaragua. Eliut is only in the sixth grade, but Samaritan's Purse workers discovered that he leads a "children's church." Each Wednesday afternoon at five o'clock, he leads a service just for children, ages 5 to 14, in the church where his father is pastor.

Eliut always starts with prayer before he reads from the Bible and gives a short message. Then other children talk about what God has done in their lives. They pray and sing songs about Jesus. At first, only about 20 children came. Now almost 60 children attend the service each week!

- Pray for Eliut as he leads children in Nicaragua to love and follow Jesus.

- Pray that you can be a witness to God's great love in your talking, in your praying, and in your singing.

Bible Verse for August

But Jesus called the little children to him and said to his followers, "Let the little children come to me. Don't stop them, because the kingdom of God belongs to people who are like these little children." Luke 18:16

How to Make a Nicaraguan Shell Frame

You will need:

- A picture frame with a plain flat border
- Seashells (enough to cover the frame you choose)
- White glue
- Glaze and brush

Step 1: Sort your shells so you can select them quickly as you work.

Step 2: Spread a light coat of glue on one side of the frame.

Step 3: Place shells on this part, one by one. Add a little more glue if needed.

Step 4: Repeat for the three other sides, one at a time.

Step 5: Let dry thoroughly.

Step 6: Cover the shells with glaze to protect them and to make them shine.

Look for the perfect picture to fit your frame!

My Prayer List

_____

_____

_____

_____

_____

_____

_____

God, Thank You For . . .

_____

_____

_____

_____

_____

_____

_____

Answers To My Prayers

_____

_____

_____

_____

SEPTEMBER

Pray for the Kids in
Kenya

Discover Kenya

Size: 219,500 square miles
(Bigger than California, smaller than Texas)
Population: 30,765,916
Capital City: Nairobi (NYE-roe-bee)

H ave you ever counted all of the grown-ups who help you? Your parents are probably at the top of the list. Then there are teachers, pastors, church youth leaders, doctors and nurses, scout leaders, coaches—and even more.

Because there has been so much sickness and death in Kenya, many kids don't have any grown-ups to love and care for them. An exciting new place is being started with the help of Samaritan's Purse—the Village of Hope. A big plot of land will have houses and gardens, schools, and medical clinics. It will be the new home for about 500 children who live on the streets and have no home. At the Village of Hope, kids will learn about Jesus, about their country and its customs, how to read and write, how to earn a living, and what is right and wrong.

As you start a new school year, keep a list of all the adults who help you for a week. You might be surprised!

- Pray for the children in Kenya who have no one to care for them.

- Pray and give thanks for your parents and the grown–ups who help you each week.

How to Make a Kenyan Fly Whisk

You will need:

- Yarn
- 4- or 5-inch stick or handle
- Masking tape or plumber's tape

Step 1: Cut 15 pieces of yarn in 24-inch lengths and fold each in half.

Step 2: Loop a short piece of string through all the cut pieces at the fold and tie it securely to one end of the stick or handle.

Step 3: Loop a 9-inch piece of yarn and tie both ends to the other end of the stick. This will be your wrist strap.

Step 4: Cover the stick from one end to the other by wrapping round and round with masking tape or plumber's tape.

Slip the wrist strap over your hand and swish those flies away!

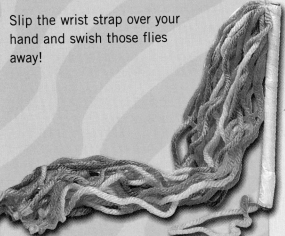

My Prayer List

_____
_____
_____
_____
_____
_____
_____
_____
_____

God, Thank You For . . .

_____
_____
_____
_____
_____
_____
_____

Answers To My Prayers

_____
_____
_____
_____

OCTOBER

Operation Christmas Child

Discover Operation Christmas Child

A project of Samaritan's Purse that delivers gift-filled shoe boxes and Christian literature to millions of children around the world each year.

A t a time of year when most boys and girls are making their Christmas lists, 10-year-old Scott made a different sort of list. His gift ideas were not for himself, but for needy children around the world.

Each year, millions of kids like Scott pack shoe boxes with small gifts—toys, candy, and other fun things—for a project called Operation Christmas Child. Samaritan's Purse delivers these boxes to children across the globe in orphanages, hospitals, refugee camps, and even garbage dumps.

Scott sent letters to friends and relatives asking for help in packing boxes and asked them to bring gifts to Thanksgiving dinner. Everyone got involved, and Scott ended up with 46 gift-filled shoe boxes. "To think about the looks on the children's faces when they open these boxes," he said, "that makes it all worth it." Turn to the back of the book to see how you can pack a shoe box, too.

- Pray that girls and boys all across the United States will want to fill shoe boxes with gifts for others.

- Pray that each shoe box will take the love of Jesus to a child far away.

Bible Verse for October

Every good and perfect gift is from above, coming down from the Father of the heavenly lights, who does not change like shifting shadows. James 1:17 (NIV)

How to Make a Christmas Card for Your Shoe Box

You will need:

- Sheet of construction paper
- Colored felt tip markers
- Your photo
- Yarn, rickrack, or sequins

Step 1: Fold paper in half and then in half again.

Step 2: Spread glue on the back of your picture and place it on the front of the card.

Step 3: Above the picture write with a felt tip marker:

This shoe box comes from (your name)

Step 4: Inside the card, write a special message or your favorite Bible verse.

Step 5: Decorate your card with yarn, rickrack, or sequins.

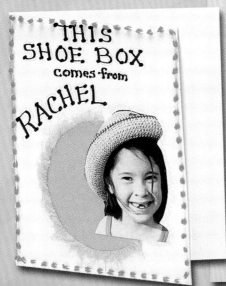

THIS SHOE BOX comes from RACHEL

My Prayer List

_____
_____
_____
_____
_____
_____
_____
_____

God, Thank You For . . .

_____
_____
_____
_____
_____
_____
_____

Answers To My Prayers

_____
_____
_____

NOVEMBER

Pray for the Kids in
Uganda

Discover Uganda

Size: 77,000 square miles
(size of Nebraska)

Population: 24,699,073

Capital City: Kampala
(kom-PAH-lah)

Can you imagine having 58 babies in one house at the same time? Well, Mama Jackie often does. She runs the Welcome Home Center in Uganda as a place to care for babies who have been orphaned or abandoned.

There are many babies in Uganda whose mothers are very poor or too sick to care for them. They are left at hospitals or found in the streets by police officers. Many of these babies are very sick, but their chances for life greatly improve if they are taken to Welcome Home. With medicines, equipment, and baby formula provided by Samaritan's Purse, Mama Jackie and her staff of Ugandan women can often help these babies to get better, but there sure are a lot of diapers to change!

- Pray for Mama Jackie and the women who help her care for tiny babies.

- Pray that more of the babies in Uganda will have loving families who can take care of them.

Bible Verse for November

With God's power working in us, God can do much, much more than anything we can ask or think of. Ephesians 3:20

How to Make a Mankala Game

You will need:

- 1 cardboard egg carton (with 12 egg-cup sections)
- Big scissors
- Poster paint or crayons
- 40 dried beans or big seeds

Step 1: Remove and discard the top off an egg carton (ask an adult to help you with cutting).

Step 2: Cut two egg cups from the carton and tape these to the center of each end of the lower part of the carton.

Step 3: Paint and decorate the lower part. Let dry.

To play:

The board is placed between two players with the long sides facing them. Each player owns the five cups in front of him or her. Four beans are placed in each of the five cups. The end cup on their right, called the mankala, will hold the players' winnings.

The player going first takes all of the beans from one of his cups and places them one by one in the cups around the board in a counter-clockwise direction. For example, if there are four beans in his cup, he places one into each of the next four cups. The other player does the same on her turn.

When a player drops the last bean of his turn into his opponent's cup, and the cup contains only two or three beans, that player wins all of the beans in the cup. The captured beans are put in the players' mankala.

The game is over when all of the beans have been captured. The player with the most beans wins!

My Prayer List

_____
_____
_____
_____
_____
_____
_____
_____

God, Thank You For . . .

_____
_____
_____
_____
_____
_____
_____

Answers To My Prayers

_____
_____
_____
_____

DECEMBER

Pray for the Kids in
Bosnia

Discover Bosnia

Size: 19,741 square miles
(about the size of Colorado)

Population: 3,964,388

Capital City: Sarajevo
(sar-uh-YAY-voe)

Eleven-year-old Aida grew up in Bosnia, a country where there once was much fighting. She had never heard of Jesus until she and her sisters received shoe box gifts two years ago from Samaritan's Purse. One of Aida's favorite gifts was a book about Jesus. She asked a worker with Samaritan's Purse to take her to church one Sunday, and she returned almost every week.

When summer came, the worker invited Aida to attend a Christian camp, and she gladly accepted. During one workshop at camp, a teacher asked the children, "Do you know who Jesus is?"

Aida stood up and said, "Yes, I know. Jesus Christ is Son of the living God, and He died and washed off my sins. Now I am clean."

- Pray for the children in Bosnia who have grown up with much fighting in their country.

- Pray for continued peace in Bosnia and that more children there will learn who Jesus is.

Bible Verse for December

That if you confess with your mouth the Lord Jesus and believe in your heart
that God has raised Him from the dead, you will be saved. Romans 10:9 (NKJV)

How to Make a Bosnian Cornhusk Doll

You will need:

- A package of dried cornhusks from a craft store
- A big package of cotton balls
- String
- Colored markers
- Yarn and glue

Step 1: Soak the dried husks in warm water for 30 minutes.

Step 2: Place cotton balls in the middle of a strip of husk, fold the long edges of the husk over the cotton balls, twist, and tie with string to make a head.

Step 3: Fold another husk and tie both ends to make arms. Slip the arms under the husks that extend from the head, and tie at the waist with string.

Step 4: Arrange overlapping husks around the waist and tie with string.

Step 5: Folding husks down, divide in two and tie for legs, or cut across to make a skirt. Let the figure dry for several hours or overnight.

Step 6: Draw a face on your doll using colored markers, or give it hair with some fuzzy yarn.

My Prayer List

_____
_____
_____
_____
_____
_____
_____
_____

God, Thank You For . . .

_____
_____
_____
_____
_____
_____
_____

Answers To My Prayers

_____
_____
_____
_____

How To Pack
A Shoe Box Gift

Here's your chance to help out a child in need!

1. Gift wrap an empty shoe box, wrapping the lid separately.
2. Fill the box with small toys, school supplies, and any other small gifts. (Please do not include war toys or items that might break, leak, melt, or spoil.)
3. Include a note and a picture of yourself, if you would like.
4. Use the Boy or Girl label provided on the next page and place it on top of your box.
5. Have your mom or dad include a check for $5 made payable to Samaritan's Purse to help cover the cost of delivery.
6. Place a rubber band around your box and lid.
7. Drop off your box at an Operation Christmas Child collection center during our annual collection week (November 17-24, 2003). Visit www.samaritanspurse.org or call 1-800-353-5949 to locate the one nearest you. You can also send your box to:
   Samaritan's Purse
   Operation Christmas Child
   801 Bamboo Road
   P.O. Box 3000
   Boone, NC 28607.
8. Most important, pray that God will bless each and every child who receives a shoe box gift.